WACKY SPORTS

By Virginia Loh-Hagan

Disclaimer: This series focuses on the strangest of the strange. Have fun reading about strange people and things! But please do not try any of the antics in this book. Be safe and smart!

45th Parallel Press

Published in the United States of America by Cherry Lake Publishing
Ann Arbor, Michigan
www.cherrylakepublishing.com

Reading Adviser: Marla Conn MS, Ed., Literacy specialist, Read-Ability, Inc.
Book Designer: Melinda Millward

Photo Credits: © Ruth Black/Shutterstock.com, cover; © Kiselev Andrey Valerevich/Shutterstock.com, 1, 12; © Aspen Photo/Shutterstock.com, 5; © D. Kucharski K. Kucharska/Shutterstock.com, 6; © Colin McPherson/Corbis/Getty Images, 7; © D. Kucharski K. Kucharska/Shutterstock.com, 8; © MehmetO/Shutterstock.com, 9; © Kingzabahojda/Dreamstime.com, 10; © ueuaphoto/Shutterstock.com, 13; © SensorSpot/iStockphoto, 14; © Emma Wood/Alamy Stock Photo, 15; © Raylipscombe/iStockphoto, 16, 17; © joyfuldesigns/Shutterstock.com, 18; © JASPERIMAGE/Shutterstock.com, 19; © Best dog photo/Shutterstock.com, 20; © Tierfotoagentur/Alamy Stock Photo, 21; © otsphoto/Shutterstock.com, 22; © simonkr/iStockphoto, 24; © fotoVoyager/iStockphoto, 25; © Martin Mecnarowski/Shutterstock.com, 26; © Camrocker/iStockphoto, 27; © Helen Filatova/Shutterstock.com, 28; © MARCEL VAN HOORN/EPA/Newscom, 29; © David Fowler/Shutterstock.com, 30

Graphic Element Credits: ©saki80/Shutterstock.com, back cover, front cover, multiple interior pages; ©queezz/Shutterstock.com, back cover, front cover, multiple interior pages; ©Ursa Major/Shutterstock.com, front cover, multiple interior pages; ©Zilu8/Shutterstock.com, multiple interior pages

45th Parallel Press is an imprint of Cherry Lake Publishing.

Library of Congress Cataloging-in-Publication Data

Names: Loh-Hagan, Virginia, author.
Title: Wacky Sports / by Virginia Loh-Hagan.
Description: Ann Arbor : Cherry Lake Publishing [2017] | Series: Stranger Than Fiction | Includes bibliographical
    references and index. | Audience: Grade 4 to 6.
Identifiers: LCCN 2017001051| ISBN 9781634728898 (hardcover) | ISBN 9781534100671 (pbk.) |
    ISBN 9781634729789 (pdf) | ISBN 9781534101562 (hosted ebook)
Subjects: LCSH: Sports—Miscellanea—Juvenile literature.
Classification: LCC GV705.4 L64 2017 | DDC 796—dc23
LC record available at https://lccn.loc.gov/2017001051

Printed in the United States of America
Corporate Graphics

About the Author

Dr. Virginia Loh-Hagan is an author, university professor, former classroom teacher, and curriculum designer. She doesn't do sports. She prefers playing piano, watching TV, and eating food. She lives in San Diego with her very tall husband and very naughty dogs. To learn more about her, visit www.virginialoh.com.

Table of Contents

Introduction

Many people love playing games. They love playing sports. They love **competing**. Competing is playing to win. They compete against others. They compete against themselves.

People play sports for fun. They play to keep active. They play to win. Some people are professional **athletes**. Athletes are really good sports players. Their job is playing sports.

All cultures have sports. There are many different sports. There are many strange sports. Some sports are stranger than strange. They're so strange that they're hard to believe. These sports sound like fiction. But they're all true!

Football and baseball are popular team sports.

chapter one

Worm Charming

The World Worm Charming Championships is in England. It started in 1980. It started at an elementary school. Principal John Bailey wrote the rules.

Three people are on a team. There's a charmer, a catcher, and a counter. Each team gets a patch of land. They charm worms to the surface. They have 30 minutes. The team with the most worms wins. Then, they return the worms to the land.

Most people use a garden fork. People stick it in the ground. They hit the garden fork. This **vibrates** the soil. Vibrate means to move back and forth. Worms come up.

Worm charmers can use any method. Some sing and dance.

Sophie Smith got a world record. She was 10 years old.
She charmed 567 worms. She did this in 2009.

chapter two

Buzkashi

Buzkashi is a Persian word. It means "goat grabbing." People grab the dead body of a headless goat. They hold it while they ride a horse. They ride at full speed. They avoid other people. They throw the goat across the goal line. Points are scored for each goal. Games can last several days.

People train their horses to ride fast. They train their horses to bite. It's a bloody sport. Many people and horses get hurt. They fall. They get bitten. They crash.

People wear heavy clothes. They wear head protection. They wear boots. They use

Buzkashi is a contact sport.

whips. They whip other people away. They carry whips
in their teeth.

Buzkashi is played all over south-central Asia. It's Afghanistan's national sport. In western China, people play on yaks.

An Afghan royal family member brought it to the United States. Men in Cleveland, Ohio, played it. They put five people on a team. They played on horseback. They played using a special ball. The ball was covered in sheepskin.

Genghis Khan may have inspired buzkashi. He was a Mongolian warrior. He lived in the 12th and 13th century. The sport trained his men for war. His men rode through towns. They grabbed loot. They grabbed animals.

The goat is soaked in cold water for 24 hours. This makes the skin tough.

Explained by Science

Aerobic exercise includes running and swimming. It makes people sweat. People's breathing speeds up. Their heart pumps more. It pumps more blood. Their blood flows faster. This shoots oxygen out to tissues. Strength training is another type of exercise. It's when people pump weight or do yoga. Muscles and bones get stronger. They bear more weight than normal. Muscles contract. They put force on bones. This force makes the bones maintain or create new tissues. There are many benefits to working out. People get healthier. They have fewer sicknesses. They have better moods. They have better memories. They think better. They have more energy. They live longer.

chapter three

Naked Rock Climbing

A new form of extreme rock climbing is naked rock climbing. These climbers don't use ropes. They don't use safety gear. They also don't wear clothes. They like feeling naked. They say it captures the "true **essence** of the climbing spirit." Essence means meaning. They feel closer to nature. Being naked makes climbing harder. It means climbers have no protection. There are more risks.

People play other naked sports. An example is the World Naked Bike Ride. The motto is "bare as you dare."

Naked rock climbing can be uncomfortable.

15

chapter four

World Gurning Contest

Gurn means to make a funny face. People stick out their lower jaw. They cover their upper lip with their lower lip. That's the most common gurn. But there are many gurns.

There's a contest for making the ugliest face. It's called the World Gurning Contest. It started in the 1200s. It started at the Egremont Crab Fair. This is in the United Kingdom.

People can't wear makeup. But they can wear fake teeth. They put their head through a horse collar. Then, they make a funny face.

Chuck is another word for gurn.

Peter Jackman is a famous gurner. He's won four times. He removed his teeth. This is so he can easily move his face.

chapter five

Cheese Rolling

Cooper's Hill is in England. It's a steep hill. People bring a wheel of cheese. The cheese weighs 7-9 pounds (3.1-4 kilograms). It's hard. People start at the top of the hill. They roll the cheese downhill. They race with the cheese. They try to catch the cheese. They race to the bottom of the hill. The first to cross the finish line wins. The prize is cheese!

Cheese can travel 70 miles (113 kilometers) per hour. It travels in different directions. It can knock people over. It can hurt people. People tumble down the hill. One year, foam cheese was used instead. This was safer. But it wasn't as much fun. People like the risks.

People watching the event get hurt, too.

chapter six

Caber Toss

A **caber** is a pole. It's made from a tree. It's about 20 feet (6 meters) long. It's 9 inches (23 centimeters) thick at one end. It's 5 inches (13 cm) thick at the other end. It weighs 175 pounds (79 kg). People throw it. This is a sport in Scotland.

Tossers throw cabers. They balance the caber. They hold it against their shoulder and neck. They crouch. They slide their hands under the caber. They lift it. They run a few steps. They toss and flip the caber. They want the caber to turn end over end. They aim to land the top near them. Tossers wear **kilts**. A kilt is a man's skirt. It's traditional Scottish clothing.

The caber toss is part of the Highland Games.

chapter seven

Ferret Legging

Ferrets are like weasels. They have sharp teeth. They have sharp claws. They're used in a strange sport. Ferret legging tests **endurance**. Endurance is how long someone can do something.

People tie their pants at the ankles. They drop two ferrets down their pants. They tighten their belts. Ferrets can't escape. People stand in front of judges. They do this for as long as they can. The winner is the last to release the ferrets.

People can't wear underwear. They wear baggy pants. Ferrets are free to roam.

Ferrets are part of the weasel family along with otters and badgers.

They can't be **sedated**. Sedated means using drugs to calm down. Ferrets must have all their teeth.

Ferrets can grip things. They do this for a long time. People can move ferrets. They do this from outside their pants.

Reg Mellor has a world record. His time is 5 hours and 26 minutes. He did this in 1981. He fed ferrets before putting them in his pants. He wore white pants. People could see the blood. Ferrets bit him. They scratched him.

Mellor practiced as a kid. He liked to hunt. Ferrets helped him hunt. Sometimes, he hunted in the rain. He kept ferrets in his pants. He kept them warm and dry. He got used to them.

The first ferret-legging record was 40 seconds.

Spotlight Biography

Metta World Peace is a strange name. He's a professional basketball player. He's an all-star. His original name is Ron Artest. He's played for several teams. Examples include the Bulls, Knicks, and Lakers. He ran a summer basketball camp. His players were in a huddle. They yelled, "World Peace." Artest liked that. He legally changed his name to Metta World Peace. He did this in 2011. He likes being creative. He wants to inspire others. *Metta* is a Buddhist word. It means wanting others to be happy

chapter eight

Yak Skiing

Yak skiing developed in India. A yak is like a cow. A skier is at the bottom of a slope. The skier is roped through a pulley to a yak. The yak is at the top of the slope. The skier shakes a bucket of nuts. This makes the yak race downhill. The yak wants the food. The skier shoots forward at top speeds.

Peter Dorje created yak skiing. He said, "Never shake the bucket of nuts before you're tied to the yak rope, though. If you shake the bucket too soon, you'll be flattened by two hairy tons of **behemoth**." Behemoth means a big beast.

The creator of yak skiing is Tibetan.

chapter nine

Dung-Spitting Contest

Hunters couldn't catch fast antelope. But they did find their **dung**. Dung is poop. Hunters had to wait. They got bored. They spit the dung to pass time. Now, dung-spitting is a sport. It began in 1994. It's played in South Africa.

People use small, hard dung pieces. They put them in alcohol. This cleans the dung. They put a piece in their mouth. They spit. They do this quickly. They don't want dung to melt in their mouth. The winner spits the farthest.

There's a yearly world championship.

Judges measure where the dung lands. Shaun van Rensburg set a world record. He did this in 2006. He spit 51.05 feet (15.6 m).

chapter ten

Goose Pulling

Goose pulling is a blood sport. There's a live goose. The goose's neck is oiled. This makes it hard to grip. The goose moves a lot. This also makes it hard to grip.

The goose's legs are hung on a pole. Or, it's hung on a rope. The rope is stretched across a road. A man rides a horse. He rushes at full speed. He tries to pull the neck off. Sometimes, another man whips at the horses. This startles the horse. It makes it even harder to grab the goose's head.

Sometimes, a hare is used instead of a goose.

The winner is able to stay in his saddle. He has the goose's head in his hand. He wins the dead bird.

The sport started in Spain. It started in the 12th century. It spread to the Netherlands, Belgium, and England. Dutch settlers brought it to the United States.

Animal rights groups don't like this sport. They try to **ban** it. Ban means to not allow. But some people still play it. However, they use a dead goose. A **vet** kills the goose **humanely**. A vet is an animal doctor. Humane means kind. Other people use ribbon instead of animals.

Goose pulling with a live goose is animal cruelty.

Try This!

- Pick a country. Research a sport from that country. Learn the sport. Play the sport. Invite friends to play.

- Be active. Do exercises. Go for a walk. Go swimming. Do yoga.

- Join a local sports league. Examples are baseball and soccer. Meet new friends. Be a good team player.

- Create your own sport. (Don't hurt any animals.) Explain how to play it. Explain the goals. Test it out. Invite friends to play. Make changes to the rules. Make the sport better.

- Walk 10,000 steps a day. Get a pedometer. This tool tracks your steps.

- Watch a sport on TV. Pick a team. Cheer for the team.

Consider This!

Take a Position! How would you define sports? How would you define hobbies? Some people think only team sports count as sports. Everything else is a hobby. Do you agree or disagree? Argue your point with reasons and evidence.

Say What? What is your favorite sport? Explain how to play. Explain what you like about the sport. Research the history of the sport. Explain the history.

Think About It! Many people don't like hurting animals. They're upset that animals are used in sports. They think it's cruel. They think it's a crime. What do you think?

Learn More!

- Agresta, Jen, ed. *Weird but True! Sports: 300 Wacky Facts About Awesome Athletics*. Washington, DC: National Geographic Children's Books, 2016.
- Gutman, Dan, and Jim Paillot (illustrator). *My Weird School Fast Facts: Sports*. New York: HarperCollins, 2016.
- Polydoros, Lori. *Strange but True Sports*. North Mankato, MN: Capstone Press, 2011.

Glossary

athletes (ATH-leets) people who are really good at sports

ban (BAN) to forbid

behemoth (beh-HEE-muth) big beast

caber (KAY-bur) long wooden pole with tapered ends

competing (kuhm-PEET-ing) playing to win

dung (DUNG) poop

endurance (en-DOOR-uhns) ability to last

essence (ES-uhns) the meaning or spirit of something

ferrets (FER-its) animals that are related to weasels

gurn (GUHRN) to make a funny face

humanely (hyoo-MANE-lee) in a kind way

kilts (KILTS) traditional Scottish attire for men; men's skirts

sedated (seh-DATE-id) calmed using drugs

tossers (TAWS-urz) people who throw something

vet (VET) animal doctor

vibrates (VYE-brates) moves back and forth

yak (YAK) an animal that is like a cow

Index